Óscar Andres Cardinal Rodriguez Maradiaga

The Challenge of Inequality
Translated by Robert H. Hopke

With an Introduction by Stefano Zamagni

A Crossroad Book
The Crossroad Publishing Company

Original publication: *Senza etica niente sviluppo*. Editrice Missionaria Italiana.
Bologna, Italy 2013

The Crossroad Publishing Company

www.crossroadpublishing.com

© 2015 The Crossroad Publishing Company

Translated from the Italian by Robert H. Hopke
Study Guide by Robert H. Hopke

This book brings together a series of articles written by Cardinal Óscar
Maradiaga that were published in the magazine *Mondo e Missione*, along with his
lectio doctoralis ("Toward an Ethics of Development") that was given on the
occasion of his honorary degree in international business and development by
the University of Parma's School of Economics, on May 10, 2013. Edited by
Emanuele Criterio, with the author's approval.

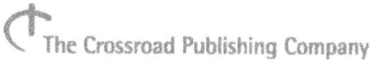

Cover design by George Foster

Library of Congress Cataloging-in-Publication Data available from the Library of
Congress.

ISBN 9780824520816

Contents

Introduction
by Stefano Zamagni

The present book by Cardinal Óscar Maradiaga offers to the reader one more melody in the chorus of talks, homilies, and pastoral letters that this notable pastor and scholar has been writing over the past few decades. The coherence that he practices in his ministry and has written about is one of his defining characteristics, and in addressing the serious and scandalous nature of the current international socioeconomic crisis, he shows that the social doctrine of the Church ought not to be limited to tending to the wounded—a necessary task, of course—but that it ought to go beyond this and tend to the deeper causes of such woundedness. If a prophet is a figure who with courage and compassion denounces what is wrong with the present and not just someone who predicts the future—after all, we have economists for that!— then Maradiaga belongs to the admittedly thin ranks of genuine prophets.

As president of Caritas International and special coordinator of the "Commission of Eight" established by Pope Francis, his starting point is a critique of the separation of Christian moral theology from economics that began in the nineteenth century with the well-known principle of "NOMA" or "non-overlapping magisterium." This notion was first formulated by Richard Whately, Anglican priest and a professor of economics at Oxford, according to whom the Church's social doctrine should have no more say over the science of economics than it should over the laws of physics or chemistry.

The great John H. Newman—now beatified—argued in vain against this NOMA principle with reason, the depth and power of which we are only now realizing. Likewise, Leo XIII tried, in *Rerum novarum cupiditas* (1891), to denounce the dangers of this principle, but his attempt was misunderstood by the very Catholic thinkers to whom it was addressed, who instead read this encyclical more as a first-aid manual written to help the poor, the exploited, and the marginalized. Clearly, there were also other ways in which it was read, but these never reached critical mass. And this is a frequent temptation within Catholic social justice movements: to intervene around the effects but fail to address any change in the causes. Nevertheless, the Franciscans of the fourteenth and fifteenth centuries did not simply provide alms to the poor of their era but took it upon themselves, despite opposition from the ecclesiastical authorities of their era, to eliminate the market economy of their society so as to pursue the common good. (Please note that "common good" is not simply "public good," and it is the former that ultimately distinguishes a civil market economy from a capitalist market economy.)

The most important message that comes through the following pages is that it is past time to weep over the horrors that we are now witnessing and to start thinking instead about the ways we might redesign the entire system of international and economic institutions that generate these injustices in the first place and are responsible for so many ways in which personal freedom is being taken away. Among many examples I do not have the space to list here, one need only think of the way the current financial-banking apparatus operates, financing the projects of a few people with the savings of many, knowing full well that it is not morally acceptable to place the financial risks associated with such projects on the backs of those people who have entrusted their financial resources to the care of these banks so as to avoid such risk. It is perfectly useless to argue about the way in which securitization—financing long-term projects with short-term resources—or the largely successful attempts to turn depositors into speculative investors on the basis of "insurance" has functioned to increase the general efficiency of the economic system: useless because the problem with these operations is not practical or technical, though many mistakes were made, but rather in the end ethical.

Everything that is technically possible is not ethically licit, unless one ascribes to Nietzsche's moral nihilism. But at this point one must have the courage to say this in the public sphere, something that has not yet happened. (Nor should one confuse what is morally licit with what is juridically legal: once the Glass Steagall Act was repealed under Clinton in 1999, Western governments raced to take advantage of this new situation in their own countries, which started the ball rolling toward the crisis of 2007.)

I attributed moral nihilism to Nietzsche above, but in fact this outlook dates back to Judas. Gospel writers Mark, Matthew, and John all see the beginning of Judas's ultimate betrayal of Jesus in the episode of Mary anointing his feet in the house of Lazarus. The very valuable perfumed oil is poured upon Jesus's body with his consent. The disciples who are there are thus witnesses to Jesus being proclaimed Messiah before them by a woman! (*Messiah* means "the anointed one.") Everyone is shocked, but only Judas has the courage to say something: "Why was this perfumed oil not sold for three hundred denarii in order to then give this money to the poor?"

Here we have the real danger of financialization. Under the "cover of money" before the disciples, Judas succeeds in making sure those around no longer "see" Jesus—the true treasure—but instead merely three hundred denarii. And like any other smart financial speculator—then as now—Judas claims that his goal is to help the poor, who, in addition to being exploited, now become instruments for a perverse rationalization of a faithless apostle. Greed, the need to have, has a mimetic power to it: it shifts our attention from true wealth—the presence of Jesus—to the illusory potential of "other alternatives." Here is the hard core of today's neo-Machiavellianism.

In the following chapters, which present a compact overview of Maradiaga's thought, a variety of perspectives are discussed—all of which, however, come together around the idea that the church's social doctrine needs to take up the challenge of addressing itself to the new social order that has come into being in the past thirty years. This challenge is to halt the advance of "Gresham's law": bad ethics drives out good ethics in our market societies, because what is "bad" may prosper in the short term, even though in the long term it may prove a failure. Therefore, we must take action so that, from short term to long term, the cost to society is not so high. How? By intervening in the structure of economic and especially financial institutions.

It is not enough—as some people continue to believe, even in Catholic circles—to count upon the virtuous behavior of individual people; we now know, empirically, why that is unrealistic. However, institutions can be held to behave virtuously in their own right; it is not true that they must be, by definition, neutral actors. Indeed, it behooves us to act quickly and decisively. The notes struck in the following pages come together in a chorus that calls us to scale the heights of what is possible and to set out upon the open sea. In this way alone can we overcome the stagnant violence of our current situation.

Globalization in Crisis

Statistics can help us understand the times in which we live. Currently more than 7 billion people are living on the earth, the highest number ever recorded. At the same time, 925 million people are suffering from hunger and starvation. In the United States alone, $50 billion was spent to feed domestic animals last year, the same amount of money that the G8 pledged in 2005 to the poorest countries in the world, a promise that has not yet been kept. In China, General Motors sells a car every twelve seconds, while every twelve seconds a child dies of starvation. Globalization has a lot of contradictions; it is complex and ambiguous.

The way in which we manage it is the key to our work and represents our responsibility to the future.

As Benedict XVI said, "Fighting poverty requires attentive consideration of the complex phenomenon of globalization."[1] There is no question that globalization is bringing into being a new world, but is it a better world? The number of people living in extreme poverty has gone down over the past three decades, yet economic inequality has increased to levels never before seen. Pope Benedict XVI, in his encyclical *Caritas in veritate*, said that "a more globalized society brings us closer but does not make us brothers" (no. 19). Globalization impacts everything: the economy, politics, cultures. All these are interconnected and reinforce one another throughout a globalized system. On the other hand, technological development and a neo-liberal economic system have brought along with them the hard reality of a gambling-casino financial market and an unregulated capitalism, where it is commonplace to place bets on securities and on the behavior of the market so as to realize profits unconnected to the real economy. But there is still another aspect of globalization, one that pertains to the global village where we are all connected to one another and therefore can influence and create change throughout the global community. Our movements have become global movements, and we have seen emerge a global citizenry. Globalization is a fact. Unlike the weather, it can be regulated and governed. But in which direction? Toward what end?

In *Caritas in veritate*, Benedict XVI says that globalization is not a negative phenomenon, but he writes, "The risk for our time is that the de facto interdependence of people and nations is not matched by ethical interaction of consciences and minds that would give rise to truly human development. Only in charity, illumined by the light of reason and faith, is it possible to pursue development goals that possess a more humane and humanizing value" (no. 9).

The Misery of the South, the Ennui of the North

Ours is an era of unprecedented changes, and yet we still live in a world full of obvious inequalities. We are creating a world in which the greed of a few is leaving the majority marginalized from history. Globalization seems more a myth than a reality. The logic of the financial markets has been globalized, and the absolutism of their capital is wreaking havoc. One might well say only the rich are globalized. Technology protects them while distancing them from the poor who must submit and work for them, since the system in many parts of the world requires poor people and keeps them in their place so that they might continue to produce on behalf of the rich.

We have not moved toward a more just system, even if that is what the marketing of "one world" promises us. Globalization is highly selective. The advantages that it produces are to the benefit of the same people as always, by way of the same distribution of wealth. It is long past time to put a halt to this scandal and to take steps toward a model of sustainability—humanizing globalization and transforming it into a genuinely universal reality.

Society is dehumanized to the extent it becomes a marketplace. Borders are indiscriminately opened for the exchange of goods and closed to people. The lack of development in many countries is producing an uncontrollable exodus of economic refugees and is leading the developed world to shut itself in behind physical and racial barriers. The urban violence of organized crime and narco-trafficking has turned Third World cities into today's jungle. Economic and social disparities divide our world between the ennui of rich countries and the subhuman life of the poor.

These days we talk a lot about quality of life, but it does not appear that globalization is generally contributing to it, for there will never been a true quality of life if we continue to fill ourselves with things, ignore the substantiality of what it means to be human, and in particular, overlook the spiritual dimension of life, which is essential to our humanity.

Living is not simply existing, but it is to exist *in a certain way*. This is what we are consistently invited to strive toward. The great Austrian psychiatrist Viktor Frankl said, "Life is not something, it is an opportunity to do something." The presence of meaning in life must be the origin of hope for the world.

Lessons from a Failed Model

The economic crisis that exploded throughout the world in 2008 and which continues even today has cast suspicion upon one of the fundamental notions of globalization: that the market would regulate itself and that a neoliberal capitalist system is ideal. In 2008 the global financial system was on the verge of collapse. The blind pursuit of profit at any cost without regard to any ethical regulation was a disaster for people and for our planet. The greedy and unsustainable lifestyle of the few created, in the words of Alan Greenspan, former head of the US Federal Reserve System, "a tsunami of credit only seen once a century."

The banks had to be bailed out. Unemployment rose. Many went out of business. Hundreds of millions of people were cast into extreme poverty. The global costs have been estimated at $25 trillion.

The crisis of 2008 is a costly, ongoing lesson we have not learned from. The global economy is yet again on the verge of falling apart. Fears of a debt crisis are spreading across the Eurozone. Financial markets are in turmoil. Growth has slowed. And in the end, the poor pay the highest price, and not only in the West. The financial contagion, austerity measures tightening aid budgets, rising tariffs impacting commercial trade—all strike at the poor in developing countries. In Asia, Vietnam and Cambodia are particularly vulnerable. And in addition to all this, the high cost of unemployment in Europe and North America means less work available for immigrant labor. The loss from emigration in Tajikistan represents 39 percent of the gross national product, 22 percent in Nepal, and 8 percent among all low-income countries.

The real fear is that we have learned the wrong lesson. Various governments have used the economic crisis as a reason to cut off aid. Aid from the main donor countries went down 3 percent in 2011—and this, in the face of the need to increase aid, which, if spent well, would yield important results. One need only look at Cambodia, where nearly all children are now going to school, thanks to investments in making primary and secondary education accessible.

Benedict XVI offered the hope that "more economically developed nations should do all they can to allocate larger portions of their gross domestic product to development aid, thus respecting the obligations that the international community has undertaken in this regard."[2]

Like communism and Nazism, any international system of organization that sacrifices the reality of human existence to blind ideology is to be condemned. Globalization has created the perception that consumption and enjoyment can be limitless. And when the means necessary to satisfy these needs diminish, then feelings of resentment and frustration grow.

A system that rewards the rich and excludes the poor creates divisions. It makes people doubt their worth, their potential, and their usefulness. Some—the weakest and most put upon—may well feel as if their very right to exist is in question. We have already seen the reaction to this system, which places the needs of 1 percent of the population ahead of the other 99 percent. We saw it in the streets of Athens, Washington, Port-au-Prince, Maputo, Mexico City, and Manila. As Pope Benedict stated, "When misery coexists alongside great wealth, a sense of injustice is born that can become a source of revolt. Thus, nations ought to take care such that social policies do not increase inequality and allow for every person to live with dignity!"[3]

If all are to participate and injustice to end, access must be provided to social, cultural, and economic opportunities, and everyone must be empowered to decide the course of their own life, from which follows the responsibility that each of us has to stand in solidarity with all others. From a Christian point of view, freedom is a right that allows every human being to live a responsible life in community. However, this is only possible within a certain set of circumstances over which individual people themselves have no control. Adequate sanitary conditions, access to education, and freedom to fulfill one's potential are such conditions. It is society's duty to put into place a secure framework for the human life of its members.

The structural and material prerequisites of such a framework are not the only aspects to be included but nonmaterial conditions as well, such as freedom from discrimination. A society's ability to provide such a framework depends on its resources. Turning again to Pope Benedict: "Considering the person to be helped first means giving them back their role as a social protagonist and permits them to take their own future in hand, to occupy their proper place in society. . . . A person's worth lies in what he *is* more than what he *has*."[4]

Economic Crisis: A Chance to Reverse the Damage

The current crisis has exposed systemic failures generated by unscrupulous speculation by a handful of people at the cost of millions of families who struggle to get by. But the crisis also presents a unique opportunity to give a new form to globalization so that it may benefit the majority. Rahm Emanuel, former White House chief of staff, said, "Let's not let a good crisis go to waste." Business and finance can work to the benefit of everyone and not just their stockholders. A return to a fair model based on collective responsibility is the key to narrowing the divide between rich and poor. We must act in such a way as to ensure that globalization and capital universally contribute to the common good.

After the 2008 economic crisis and the bailout of the banks, the pope said, "The world has witnessed the vast resources that governments can draw upon to rescue financial institutions deemed 'too big to fail.' Surely the integral human development of the world's peoples is no less important: here is an enterprise, worthy of the world's attention, that is truly 'too big to fail.'"[5] I'm told that in Taiwan they have a saying, "A cow led off to Beijing is a still a cow," which means that someone with a bad habit has a hard time changing their behavior, regardless of their circumstances. It is also said that "the fish rots from the head down." Rich countries have led the world into a capitalism without regulation and are responsible for bringing the whole world to the brink of disaster twice within five years. Poor countries should not expect the West to behave in a responsible fashion and ought to act, now, on their own, to move toward the greater good.

If the sun is setting in the West, it is rising in the East. In 1820 Asia represented two-thirds of the global economy. With Western industrialization, Asian countries have now experienced two centuries of steady decline. Today, this trend is reversed. The rapid growth of many Asian countries beginning in 1950 is one of the greatest success stories of development in recent history.

Half a century ago, South Korea, Indonesia, and Malaysia had levels of poverty on par with other developing countries. Taiwan, for example, had a standard of living similar to that of Zambia in 1950, as gauged by its gross domestic product. Fifty years later, the GDP of Zambia is the same, while that of Taiwan is thirty-two times greater. The percentage of people in eastern Asia living on less than one euro per day dropped to 14 percent in 2008 from 77 percent in 1981. In the last five years, the number of people in Asia living in poverty dropped by 430 million.

This century may well see something on the order of 3 billion people in Asia achieve the same standard of living as people in European countries, with Asia perhaps producing fully one-half of the world's gross international product by the year 2050. Some might say that this success is due to the free market. This is partly true; as South Korea and Taiwan have shown us, by providing labor and opening their business to foreign investment, they are protecting the most developed of their own industries and providing them the space to become engines of growth. In other words, they employ protectionist policies when it suits them, just as the West places value on a "free market" above all others.

Growth in Asia is impressive but uneven. Economic prosperity is not reaching the poorest people in those countries. This area of the world's most rapid economic growth is still where half of the world's population lives in extreme poverty. Five hundred million Asians do not have secure access to drinking water. In India, Indonesia, and China, the gulf between rich and poor has grown in the past two decades, and millions of people have been left behind. In India and China, the difference in income between the top 10 percent of the population and the bottom 10 percent of the population is 50 to 1. One-fifth of their GDP is in the hands of 5 percent of their population, while the poor are denied fair access to education, health care, and other services. The child of a poor family is ten times more likely to die at birth than the child of an affluent family.

Humanity as Family: A Dream or a Practical Possibility?

"One human family, zero poverty" was the theme of a recent Caritas International general assembly. Taiwan had a great deal to teach us about reaching this goal, since only 1 percent of its population lives in poverty, which an analyst suggested might well be the lowest percentage ever achieved in all of human history. But even there, the crisis of the last few years has exacted a price.

The globalized economy always seems to create winners and losers, exacerbating the inequalities that exist. We cannot accept any political or social system in which the rich exploit the poor. Our challenge is to build a world of brotherhood, in which we live together as one family in peace. Globalization is nothing new for the Catholic Church, of course. Our church is one universal people united in sacrament and solidarity. Concern for social justice and human rights is obviously not the only task of the church, but it is an essential part of it and an indispensible dimension of *koinonia*. The challenges ahead of us are real and sometimes discouraging. In the crisis we are now passing through, certain statements bring light and hope and encourage us to use globalization for uniting all of humanity into one family.

The papal encyclical *Spes salvi* says, "The true measure of humanity is essentially determined in relationship to suffering and to the sufferer. This holds true both for the individual and for society. A society unable to accept its suffering members and incapable of helping to share their suffering and to bear it inwardly through 'com-passion' is a cruel and inhuman society" (no. 38).

When we say, "Our Father, who art in heaven," we pray with the whole human family. Jesus's prayer becomes our own, and it is the prayer of every single individual as a brother or sister in Christ as members of the whole human family. In this one prayer we make real our faith, and we share it universally. If we human beings are a family, we cannot allow there to be a Second, Third, or Fourth World. This is nonnegotiable. We cannot allow one brother or sister to be lost, lest we fail at our own call to salvation. If we seek to channel the forces of globalization toward this end, indeed our only motto can be, "One human family, zero poverty."

The Rights and Duties of a Common Destiny

To choose justice and to overcome poverty require a revision of priorities for countries and for politics. One does not need a whole lot of theory to know the direction in which we should be moving. Providing for basic needs, both "active" and "passive," are what we call the "common good," a phrase politicians seeking election to "public service" tend to use even if, in the end, in many cases, they end up only serving their own good and not the public's.

Human beings have basic needs that are of a "passive" nature, and for these, the state cannot fail to be of assistance. These are food, health, clothing, and housing—the things upon which life depends and which should be the starting point for an examination of political conscience on the part of a government and of a social conscience on the part of a community. These conditions are the basis for justice and the place where one begins to overcome poverty.

Generally, we take issue with violence in the world. We create international courts of justice to punish genocide or international violations of human rights, but the number of persons dying of hunger in our world far outstrips those killed by machine guns or those who died in the concentration camps of the past (Nazi or Soviet) or the present (refugee camps), or in ethnic ghettos. Here, second-class citizens watch us pass them by, satisfied with our lives and yet full of fear due to the insecurity that inevitably results from the "subversiveness of poverty." Such insecurity is understandable in people who, after all, cannot just allow themselves to die without struggling to survive within a globalized society—a society that, instead of encouraging responsibility, sacrifices them and refuses to acknowledge that every responsibility that it shirks represents a family condemned to death.

The duties of the state are the rights of its citizens, and we are seeing more and more how the state is failing in its task of preserving and promoting life, food, health, and housing. We are obligated to put a halt to this failure, and we are doing this by way of the substructures of civil society—nongovernmental organizations, charitable foundation, community organizations—that refuse to allow their aims to be compromised and by means of those political parties that, having recognized and in some cases corrected their previous mistakes, have undergone an internal reorientation toward realizing the common good.

But beyond these basic necessities, there are needs of an "active" nature, those that promote the participation of every citizen, including the poor, through "training and education" and "taking responsibility" for fulfilling one's potential.

To create a society that moves forward in knowledge, it is necessary to put in motion a world wherein human beings can work and feel themselves as co-creators of the society in which they live. Illiteracy must be overcome, of course, for only millionaires have the luxury of illiteracy; a poor person without training or employment is condemned from the start to an undeserved fate. Jacques Attali, in his book on the history of the future[6] calls us to avoid, through injustice or hunger, putting ourselves—and our children and our grandchildren—in the midst of an implacable struggle between a "sedentary" urban population in our cities and a "nomadic" people besieging and sacking these cities in their frantic attempt to survive. We live between fear and hope, but I am sure it is not too late. We must dream with our eyes open. The freshness of a new spirit cannot be denied.

Toward an Ethic of Development

I would like to speak about ethics in a world, today's world, which is facing the greatest crisis we have seen since 1929. It is true that we have faced many other hard times over the years—for example, during the 1960s—but nothing as troubling as the situation we are living through today.

I would like to talk about ethics because every great economic or political crisis has been associated with the failure of certain principles, by the reinforcement of certain values, and by an inability to establish the true value of things. Here I'm thinking of the "liquid society" that sociologist Zygmunt Bauman spoke of, or the relativism that Benedict XVI and many other brilliant minds have denounced, so that we might go beyond fanaticism and fundamentalism.

Today's human beings are, on the one hand, technical giants, and on the other like newborn babies when it comes to ethics. The power that we wield, in either technical or scientific terms, is indisputable, yet this power is problematic, deployed as it is within a context of confusion concerning to what end it is being used. Our capability of *how* runs into our lack of clarity about *why* or *how come*, since what is possible is not necessarily appropriate or suitable for human beings.

The technical "yes, we can" needs the ethical discernment of "yes, we must" on the human level. In other words, the human factor—that is, all that contributes to the full realization of an individual's potential as a member of society and all the groups and communities within that society—is the obligatory and indispensible point of reference for any technical possibility that claims to be human in nature.

The field of ethics is the questioning of human perception in every situation that has an impact on the person and on society. The terms *human* or *inhuman* represent ethical criteria that undergird every action affecting human dignity and solidarity or that reject any action that harms or injures this dignity and solidarity.

We have now passed the year 2015 the target date set back in the year 2000 by the General Assembly of the United Nations for realizing its famous Millennium Development Goals, but there is now so much uncertainty in the world economy that, despite all the effort spent from 2000 until now, many people believe these goals cannot be reached. Still others wonder how we might even come to an *economicist* view of development at all.

The theory of development is in its infancy. Due to the need to rebuild society and the economy after the devastation of World War II,

this new theory came about as a reaction to economic models that were unable to ensure con-
stant, consistent growth toward the well-being
of all countries. There is no doubt that, in the
past fifty years, the economy has been a greater
object of focus in the field of social sciences,
given its enormous influence on public policy
intended to foster growth and reduce poverty.

In 2000 the United Nations Development
Programme (UNDP), in its examination of the
failure of development policies in the majority of poor countries as well of the measures
undertaken by international institutions and
agencies, in its annual report[7] arrived at the
conclusion that "the instruments used to assess
poverty as fixed by the 1995 World Summit for
Social Development are based upon monetary
measures, while most experts on development
agree that poverty is not simply a matter of
income but is a multidimensional reality. For
these reasons, countries need to begin to in-
corporate in their respective programs against
poverty indices of human development such as

the reduction of malnutrition, increase in literacy and life expectancy."

This approach is linked to the concept of development that UNDP had introduced and promoted in its 1990 report,[8] after having recognized the limits inherent in using statistics that measured income and the growth of gross domestic product, stating categorically that income was not the sum total of a human life and proceeding then to define development in terms of the opportunities people have for realizing their full human potential: "Human development is a process of broadening the range of choices that people have, a broad range of options, the most important of which are a long and healthy life, the possibility of an education, access to the resources needed for a respectable standard of living, to which must be added civil liberties, the protection of human rights, and self-respect." Later, UNDP stated that "development has two aspects to it: the formation of human capacities and the possibility for their expression. If the development of individuals is unsuccessful in bringing these two aspects into harmony with one another, then the individual is apt to experience considerable frustration."

If the economic aspect is reconsidered, then most certainly there will be repercussions in how the overall concept of development itself is understood. One of the causes of the problems is pointed out by economist Amartya Sen whose notion can be summed up as follows. Every economic problem has two dimensions—*technical/engineering*, which is concerned with understanding with what means one might use to achieve immediate, concrete objectives in production, distribution, and consumption; and *ethical*, which is concerned with the ultimate end of any economic action and of the economy as a whole. Ethics considers issues connected to human motivation and explores the following questions: How should we, how must we live? To what purpose are the efforts people pour into their work?

Neither wealth nor growth in production and income are justifications in themselves, if there are not means to achieve other objectives. It is unreasonable to seek to achieve economic growth at all costs when the purpose and motivations for doing so are unclear. If the economy drives political decision-making without taking into account both dimensions that Sen described, the technical and the ethical, then those decisions are irrational. There is no question that the nearly exclusive focus on the technical dimension, which represents an important aspect of the science of economics, has considerably enriched this field of study and has led to understanding very concrete problems in economic relationships, especially problems that have to do with how markets function. This analysis, in fact, has been so useful that indeed the common perception of the economy is that its sole purpose is to resolve these types of issues.

The problem with this one-sided view lies, however, in the fact that by ignoring the ethical dimension of the economy, we likewise ignore the whole set of values that make life human. Instead, we are given a theoretical and abstract approximation that in turn has a much too simplistic effect on our institutions and our society, and we forget the human part of the picture.

The growing distance between these two dimensions of the economy, besides being evidence of a break with the original focus of this scientific discipline, has led to an impoverishment of the field and a loss of direction in technical discussions. This explains in part why research in development, carried out from within the dominant view of economics, so often confuses development with *growth*, which is a technical concept and represents only one part of development as whole, and thus impedes a fuller view of development. By meeting the challenge presented by a limited view—a challenge inherent in the scientific study of the economy—we would be better equipped to handle the problem of development.

A new perspective, used to grasp development as a whole, could open up connections with other basic understandings of what it means to live as a human being in the world, concepts such as quality of life, excellence, and fulfill-ment. Starting with Sen's observations, one can take steps forward to understand more precise-ly the process of development and thus bring in the ethical dimension. Asking ourselves what our objectives and goals are, the *why* of devel-opment, is crucial. A process or a strategy for development is then considered promising or not in relationship to the worth and dignity of life's meaning.

From the ethical standpoint, the central ques-tion is, "What is development *for*?" Indeed, sim-ply asking the question keeps us from taking for granted that development is defined merely as economic growth or as aspiring to the level of affluence achieved in the last century by those countries with the greatest economic growth and largest accumulation of material goods.

What Is Development For?

Just as it is not easy to answer the ques-tion, "What is development and what are its purposes?" neither is it easy to determine what a worthwhile, desirable life would be, particularly taking into account the various ways that human beings understand happiness, cultural differences, and various philosophies of life.

Many ethicists of development have agreed—in order to avoid endless discussion—to try to come to a basic synthesis of specific overlapping areas, noting in a general way where cultures and differing perspectives converge on certain essential characteristics of a "worthwhile life." Out of these efforts have been identified three *values* that are sought out, ideally, as the objectives or ends of all people and societies, representing what all cultures consider a "worthwhile life."

These three basic values are sustenance, respect, and freedom. These ends are understood by the research as universal in an intrinsic sense, despite the fact that their mode of implementation may vary according to place and time and that their relationship to one another may vary as well. Denis Goulet, theoretician of human development, presents the content of each of these values in the following way.

All people consider a worthwhile life one in which one can *maintain and improve one's quality of life.* The value here lies in the function of life itself, not in its origin nor in its rarity nor in the content of work that people might find meaningful. Thus, it is easy to identify underdevelopment when there is a lack of basic means for sustaining life, such as food, medicine, housing, and adequate physical protection.

Another element of a worthwhile life is *respect*: each person respected as a worthy human being, and not to be used as a mere instrument in the service of achieving someone else's aims. Everyone, in every society, seeks to be respected, seen, valued, honored, and recognized, "to appear in public without shame," in the words of Adam Smith. And this is not just a quality of individuals but also the expectation of groups. Poor, "underdeveloped" societies, despite their own self-respect, suffer in comparison to societies that are more advanced economically and technologically, because nowadays, prosperity and wealth have become the sole criteria for valuing an individual or a community.

From here is born the longing for development within many societies, Goulet explains, as well as the resistance that certain peoples have to the changes that a "model of development" would impose upon them. When material well-being is seen as essential aspect of one's worth, it becomes very hard for "underdeveloped" countries to feel respected until or unless they reach a specific level of growth, which then leads to the danger of throwing themselves into seeking material wealth and legitimizing development, understood simplistically as growth, as an end in itself, as a way of earning respect. In other cases, this authentic need to feel respected becomes the reason that some societies resist and reject development. If an intervention used by an agent of development humiliates a community, self-respect will lead that community to reject such changes.

Freedom is the third component of this general concept of a worthwhile life, which so-called developed countries value as much as "developing" countries. Here, too, the meaning of this word is given differing interpretations, though in the end all of these come together in the idea that freedom means being able to count on a wide range of alternatives for living within a society as well as the possibility of choosing between them.

These three values are part of every dimension of human life. In particular, Goulet uses the image of a flower to bring together the six dimensions of human life that are necessary in any definition of development: cultural, ecological, economic, social, political, and "meaningfulness" or "fulfillment," the last here addressing one's connection with the transcendent.

Ethics and Economy: Two Inseparable Dimensions

The question of the "purpose" of development and a possible cross-cultural agreement concerning the essential characteristics of this purpose does not exhaust the process of an ethical examination of development. Certain important aspects of development also must be considered when elaborating a new model of development.

Ethics and the economy cannot be separated, insofar as they each, certainly, move forward as rational processes and not simply as the result of voluntary subjective action. Only by proceeding in a coherent way with respect to the

47

scientific nature of the economy and the norms proper to ethics will it be possible to simultaneously reach the goals of efficiency and justice, productivity and equity, competition and solidarity, within an integrated development of social organization and shared human existence.

For this reason, the definition of these objectives and their implementation through development strategies and policies must be the result of collective efforts, since no one, not even a legitimately elected government, can make decisions alone on behalf of others. The moral content of these decisions concerning every objective and every measure proposed in favor of development depends on whether the decision has been reached with full awareness of all the different possible alternatives available in any given situation. At the same time, these decisions must also be examined with regard to their potential impact on society, on particular social groups, as well as on the "whole household" and on the environment.

These, therefore, are decisions that are made when economic policies are being formulated. The ethics of any given development plan, strategy, or policy requires the following steps: the participation of all affected by any concrete action; comprehensive contribution to the scientific and social analysis so as to identify technically realizable alternatives; the identification of general, common interests among all parties so as to direct these concrete actions; and space for adequate, inclusive, equitable, and reciprocal discussion. The result of such a process would then be the basis for truly legitimate decision making on the part of those in charge.

A New Model of Development

While a social-scientific analysis of specifically economic problems focuses on the technical level of solution, an integral resolution of these issues may, after all, be unattainable or at least undesirable for any given society as a whole. An ethical analysis opens up a broader horizon of study by introducing a component of reason that will not allow the question of *how* to be separated from the question of *to what end*.

From this point of view, ethics are not external to the problems of the economic, social, political, or generally human order. They are a constitutive dimension, intrinsic to any integral understanding of any human issue or action undertaken. Certainly what is considered "important" varies across societies and cultures. In fact, every society, at whatever time in history, produces its own ethical perspective, its own definition of values. Such variability makes it complicated (but not impossible) to tease out common and essential elements from the range of cultural variations so as to formulate certain basic aims of all development. According to certain anthropological studies and ethical analyses of development, these aims would be: to provide all groups with a minimum basic standard for what a "worthwhile life" entails, to provide in the best and broadest way the means for the sustenance of all members of a society, to create and improve the material conditions of life in relationship to a sense of perceived respect, and finally, to liberate all people from any form of oppression.

It is important, though, not to confuse such aims with notions about a "quality of life" in the so-called developed countries, where the question *to what purpose*, with regard to development, remains open and where each country must find an answer in its own way.

Our currently accepted concept of development—which looks at "economic growth" as the priority above all others—is not adequate to measure such broader and more integral objectives. In the common life lived out within a society, the concrete way in which *to what purpose* gets translated into plans, strategies, and policies designed to foster development would require the use of rational analysis so as to articulate the ethical along with the social-scientific, economic, and political through a participatory process that democracy supports.

On the whole and in each specific case, the intervention of ethics enriches and broadens the concept and analysis of development. Multiculturalism and a plurality of popular identities have been compromised by the explosion of a market that is only interested in a homogeneous culture of hedonism and frantic consumption, such that the meaning of life is lost in this search to possess and enjoy, all while millions of people in the world suffer from hunger and malnutrition, a lack of education and health care, and live within conditions of structural violence devoid of all compassion.

The market, as a mechanism of exchange, has been transformed into an instrument of this culture. Many observers have noted that the materially ambitious and even invasive logic of the market has reduced the area available to the larger human community for voluntary, public action at all levels. The market imposes its own way of thinking and acting and establishes a range of value that then dictates behavior. Those crushed by it often see globalization as a tidal wave of destruction that threatens social norms and elements of culture that have, up until now, given direction to life.

It is fundamental, therefore, to apply ethical discernment as a criterion in evaluating globalization and to base this evaluation on two inseparable principles. The first, as John Paul II put it, is "the inalienable value of the human person, source of all human rights and every social order."[9] The human being must always be an end, and never a means, a subject and never an object nor a commercial product. The second is the value of human culture, which no external power has the right to diminish or destroy. Globalization cannot be a new form of colonialism.

The diversity of cultures must be respected, and this respect should set the tone for a life of universal harmony among the peoples of the world. In particular, attention must be paid to that which deprives the poor of what is precious to them, including their beliefs and religious practices, given that true religious conviction is the clearest manifestation of human freedom. Politics, it would seem, is optional. In a democratic state, the citizens, their enterprises, and their organizations within a society in general have an obligation to participate, not just in election, but in public life as a whole, as part of planning for, discussion concerning, and the control of public affairs.

Certainly business owners are acting politically in the best sense of the word when they help their countries by remaining there to create employment, to invest in the building up of infrastructures, trusting in a future of peace, growth, social justice, and cooperation, so that all might live a worthwhile life. This is the role of ethics in the economy.

Life in the Center

In *Caritas in veritate*, Benedict XVI put forward the idea of a "human ecology" that transcends a dualism too often encountered up to now: the separation of an ethics of life from an ethics of the environment. In Paragraph 28 he writes, "One of the most striking aspects of development in the present day is the important question of respect for life, which cannot in any way be detached from questions concerning the development of peoples," after which he goes on to mention infant mortality, population control, laws contrary to the sanctity of life, and an "anti-birth" mentality that is often portrayed "as if it were a form of cultural progress." The encyclical enunciates quite clearly a principle that seems to have been forgotten: "Openness to life is at the center of true development."

Further on, in Paragraph 48, he continues to address our care for the environment, a subject to which Benedict XVI referred so frequently as to earn himself the media title of the "green pope." He writes, "Today the subject of development is also closely related to the duties arising from our relationship to the natural environment. The environment is God's gift to everyone, and in our use of it we have a responsibility toward the poor, toward future generations, and toward humanity as a whole." As believers, we are obliged to recognize in nature the wonderful fruit of God's creative action, to be used responsibly so as to meet legitimate needs while respecting the balance of nature itself.

As prophets for life, we insist that the use of natural resources on the part of economic groups cannot be allowed to hold sway at the expense of individual nations and humanity as a whole and destroy the source of life itself. Future generations have a right to receive a habitable world and not a planet being suffocated by atmospheric toxicity. "If this vision is lost, we end up either considering nature an untouchable taboo or, on the contrary, abusing it. Neither attitude is consonant with the Christian vision of nature as the fruit of God's creation."

The earth is a gift from the Creator to be "cared for and cultivated," but it is not more important than the human person. The pope reminds us that on earth there is room for all people, but we must also undertake to leave the earth in a condition suitable for subsequent generations to live here. In Paragraph 49, he states that this duty implies taking on the task of living together in such a way as to reinforce the alliance between human beings and our environment, and it is desirable for the international community and individual governments to act effectively in limiting any use of the environment that might be harmful.

Never before has it been more important to help people to see in creation more than simply a source for wealth creation or human exploitation. Paragraph 51 tells us that "the way humanity treats the environment influences the way it treats itself, and vice versa." Such reciprocity is often not considered in our modern society. Desertification and the loss of farmland are also the result of the impoverishment of its people and their lack of education.

The Church has a responsibility toward creation that must be publicly asserted, not just to defend earth, air, and water as gifts of the Creator given to all but to keep human beings from destroying themselves. This would be a truly human ecology. "In order to protect nature, it is not enough to intervene with economic incentives or deterrents; not even an apposite education is sufficient. These are important steps, but the decisive issue is the overall moral tenor of society. If there is a lack of respect for the right to life and to a natural death; if human conception, gestation, and birth are made artificial;

if human embryos are sacrificed to research, the conscience of society ends up losing the concept of human ecology and, along with it, that of environmental ecology."

We Need *Human* Development

Our times require urgent reflection on issues of justice and poverty. If we choose not to think about or deal with these issues, we do a disservice to future generations who may well look back and consider it their own grave misfortune to have had ancestors incapable of dedicating themselves in solidarity and clarity to the transformation of the world from what it is to what we would like it to be. Generally, we think of youth as the age of dreams and of maturity as the age of realization. But this way of thinking is changing. We are all called, at every age, to dream and accomplish those dreams. If the culture of globalization brings with it any good at all, it can be found in the idea that a dream is valid only when it takes shape in fact. For this to happen, individualism must be set aside. In the words of a beautiful Brazilian song, "Whoever dreams stays in the land of dreams but whoever dreams with others creates new realities."[10]

In today's world a false optimism about globalization is circulating, such that one is labeled a pessimist when, even though appreciating certain aspects, one questions the choices being made and raises the possibility of negative consequences. What place does the human being have in the current forms of globalization? This is the basic question. We must ask ourselves if we are all a part of humankind or if—having overcome the division of white from black, indigenous from *conquistadores*—we are creating now an insuperable barrier between rich and poor, individually and in society.

Forced migration is an example of terrible poverty that can no longer be hidden. Migrants suffer from total exclusion, having even lost their territorial rights. Every day, thousands of people risk their lives in search of a place where they might earn a living to survive, and they do so because they have nothing left to lose.

Europe and North America are seeing migrants come from all over the world, even China, as Beijing looks down from on high at its own citizens who are emigrating. Contemporaneously, and for the same reason, internal migration of the poor within Latin America is growing as well. Impoverished areas around major and medium-size cities continue to grow, and often these migrants trade the desperation caused by true poverty for a fleeting mirage based on an even more terrible hope. The cynical rationalization one so frequently hears— that people have always yearned to move to the big city in such of culture and opportunity—can really no longer be accepted on its face. Displacement is not tourism, and mass immigration is not "poor people traveling to see the world."

To change this state of affairs, we must go beyond the perversity of those who read the parable of the rich man and Lazarus and yet refuse to increase the number of those dining while still holding the opinion that the rich man ought to eat more and better, those who believe that the number and quality of the crumbs falling from his table will increase for those poor Lazaruses living in indigence, exclusion, and underdevelopment. As a church, we have tried to call attention to the barrier between rich and poor, but we have not yet been successful in moving governments or those larger organizations in charge of international society. We need a sustainable form of human development and a world in which a life of worth can be lived. For this reason, all models of society and all collective action must clearly put human beings at the center of its design.

Guide for Sharing, Prayer, and Practice

These four themes capture the core ideas in these reflective essays. They are themes that we believe will elicit discussion and the sharing of different perspectives.

Globalization

1. Cardinal Maradiaga contrasts certain positive aspects of globalization with other negative aspects of this phenomenon. In what ways has your own life been improved or helped by globalized communications or connec-

tions, and in what ways has this phenomenon had a negative impact on you or your family?

For prayer and practice:

"Economic and social disparities divide our world between the ennui of rich countries and the subhuman life of the poor." Direct your prayer today toward discerning ways in which God may be calling you to either greater detachment from material abundance or toward helping those in material need around you.

2. How has your experience of the Catholic Church been global? Discuss ways in which you have directly experienced the Church as "one universal people united in sacrament and solidarity."

For prayer and practice:

The focus of prayer that the author suggests here is the first phrase of the Lord's Prayer, the universal prayer of the Christian family. Take some time to be quiet, concentrate on your breath, and breathe in slowly and out slowly, taking each one of these six words, "Our . . . Father . . . who . . . art . . . in . . . heaven," one at a time, one each for every inhalation and exhalation, so you have the time to let the Lord work through the meaning of every one of them. If inspired to do so, pray the whole prayer this way, breathing in and breathing out on every individual word.

Inequality

The author quotes Pope Benedict's observation and counsel: "When misery coexists alongside great wealth, a sense of injustice is born that can become a source of revolt. Thus, nations ought to take care such that social policies do not increase inequality and allow for every person to live with dignity!"

What social policies on the international, national, state, or local level do you think foster inequality, and which policies do you think move toward providing life with dignity?

For prayer and practice:

Take time to think about the social or economic inequalities you seen around you in your everyday life and then pray for the Lord to open your eyes to these disparities in ways you may not have before.

Ethics

The author challenges us to think about our economic lives in an ethical fashion. Do you face ethical challenges in your own economic life?

For prayer and practice:

The key to living an ethical life is to align our behavior with our values, and for Christians, those values are often best discerned in the life Jesus lived among us and in the message of the gospel he preached. Take some quiet time today and let your mind wander prayerfully on whatever episode in the life of Christ seems to occur to you. What is the value He incarnated? And how might you live that value more fully?

Responsibility

"Today the subject of development is also closely related to the duties arising from our relationship to the natural environment. The environment is God's gift to everyone, and in our use of it we have a responsibility toward the poor, toward future generations, and toward humanity as a whole," writes Pope Benedict. Discuss what you feel is your God-given duty toward the poor, toward future generations, and toward humanity as a whole.

For prayer and practice:

As one person, it may be hard, if not overwhelming, to think about ways in which any one of us can affect such large and universal issues on the world stage as are presented in this book on globalization. Allow your prayer today, as you finish reading this book, to be a prayer of revelation. How is God calling you to act in your own life, as you let this larger perspective inform and shape your thoughts, feeling, and spirituality?

Notes

1 Benedict XVI, "Message for the Celebration of the 42nd World Day of Peace," January 1, 2009.

2 Benedict XVI, *Caritas in veritate*, paragraph 60.

3 Benedict XVI, "Address to the Ambassadors of the Holy See of Ethiopia, Malaysia, Ireland, Fiji, and Armenia," May 5, 2012.

4 Ibid.

5 Benedict XVI, Meeting with the Representatives of British Society, Westminster Hall, September 17, 2010.

6 J. Attali, *Brief History of the Future* (Fazi, 2009).

7 *Human Development Report 2000, no. 11: Human Rights* (Rosenberg & Sellier, 2000).

8 *Human Development Report 1990, no. 1: How It Is Defined? How It Is Measured* (Rosenberg & Sellier, 2000).

9 John Paul II, "Address to the Participants of the Plenary of the Pontifical Academy of the Social Sciences," April 27, 2011.

10 Raul Seixas, "Sonho que se sonha só."

CHURCH AT THE CROSSROAD
A SERIES OF GLOBAL MARKING POSTS

Leonardo Boff
Toward an Eco-Spirituality

In this engaging brief, the author outlines a new vision for human stewardship of the earth. This is an ideal first step to take for individuals and groups to study ecology in a Christian context, and to understand that ecology is no longer a luxury for a few, but an imperative for everyone working for a more just world.

ISBN 978-0-8245-2076-2
pb / 100 pages

Support your local bookstore or order directly from the publisher at www.CrossroadPublishing.com.

To request a catalog or inquire about quantity orders, please e-mail sales@CrossroadPublishing.com.

The Crossroad Publishing Company

CHURCH AT THE CROSSROAD
A SERIES OF GLOBAL MARKING POSTS

Philip Jenkins
The New Map of the Global Church

By 2025, 75 percent of Catholics in the world will be non-European; the new global church will have its center of gravity in Latin America, Asia, and Africa. This fascinating brief explores the metamorphosis taking place in the global community of believers.

ISBN 978-0-8245-2078-6
pb / 100 pages

Support your local bookstore or order directly from the publisher at www.CrossroadPublishing.com.

To request a catalog or inquire about quantity orders, please e-mail sales@CrossroadPublishing.com.

The Crossroad Publishing Company

THE POPE FRANCIS RESOURCE LIBRARY

**Diego Fares, Foreword by
Antonio Spadaro, SJ**
The Heart of Pope Francis

*How a New Culture of Encounter Is
Changing the Church and the World*

A presentation of what lies at the heart of Pope Francis's pontificate: a keen interest in people and a passion for understanding the life experience of others. Written by his longtime friend and fellow Jesuit, this book clarifies the underlying thoughts and choices Jorge Bergoglio has made throughout his life in developing a culture of encounter that he now proposes as the basis for the rebirth of the whole church, and the world.

ISBN 978-0-8245-2074-8
hc / 100 pages

*Support your local bookstore or order directly from the publisher at
www.CrossroadPublishing.com.*

*To request a catalog or inquire about quantity orders,
please e-mail sales@CrossroadPublishing.com.*

The Crossroad Publishing Company

About the Author

Óscar Andrés Rodríguez Maradiaga, SDB, is a Honduran cardinal of the Catholic Church. He is the archbishop of Tegucigalpa, the president of Caritas Internationalist, and the former president of the Latin American Episcopal Conference. He worked as the Vatican's representative to the World Bank and the International Monetary Fund and has spoken out on social justice and inequality for many decades.

About the Translator

Robert H. Hopcke is the author of numerous works in the field of Jungian psychology and Roman Catholic spirituality. He has translated a variety of books in fields as diverse as art history, sexuality and religion, including most recently, with Paul A. Schwartz, *The Little Flowers of St. Francis*, from Shambhala Publications.

About the Publisher

The Crossroad Publishing Company publishes CROSSROAD and HERDER & HERDER books. We offer a 200-year global family tradition of books on spiritual living and religious thought. We promote reading as a time-tested discipline for focus and understanding. We help authors shape, clarify, write, and effectively promote their ideas. We select, edit, and distribute books. Our expertise and passion is to provide wholesome spiritual nourishment for heart, mind, and soul through the written word.